U0361612

（中英对照）

艺术的二十二个遐想

22 Reflections on Art

李　睦　著

清华大学出版社
北京

图书在版编目（CIP）数据

艺术的二十二个遐想：汉英对照/李睦著. —北京：清华大学出版社，2021.10（2022.12重印）
ISBN 978-7-302-59006-4

Ⅰ.①艺…　Ⅱ.①李…　Ⅲ.①美育－文集－汉、英　Ⅳ.①G40-014

中国版本图书馆CIP数据核字（2021）第176423号

责任编辑：纪海虹
封面设计：闻达文化
责任校对：王荣静
责任印制：丛怀宇

出版发行：清华大学出版社
　　　　　　网　　址：http：//www.tup.com.cn，http：//www.wqbook.com
　　　　　　地　　址：北京清华大学学研大厦A座　　邮　　编：100084
　　　　　　社 总 机：010-83470000　　　　　　　　邮　　购：010-62786544
　　　　　　投稿与读者服务：010-62776969，c-service@tup.tsinghua.edu.cn
　　　　　　质量反馈：010-62772015，zhiliang@tup.tsinghua.edu.cn
印 装 者：三河市东方印刷有限公司
经　　销：全国新华书店
开　　本：130mm×205mm　　**印　　张：**3.625　　**字　　数：**67千字
版　　次：2021年10月第1版　　　　　　**印　　次：**2022年12月第2次印刷
定　　价：38.00元

产品编号：090767-01

木 2016.7.

自　序

　　本书是我在过去较长一段时间里陆续写出的，其中几篇的写作时间相对更早一些。这些先后流露在纸面上的遐想都与自己曾经的艺术教育经历密切相关，所以取名"遐想"。在教学和创作中想到些事情很重要，想到以后再写出来就更重要，否则就等于没想。但是此书的出版还有着另外一个有趣的原因：书稿的译者克莱尔是我多年的老朋友，长期居住在法国。她热爱艺术，研究中国文化，比较了解我的创作思路和艺术教学，她仔细阅读过我写的文字，并且将其中一部分译成英文。为此，她付出了非常大的努力，她的品格和才能始终令我敬佩。也正因如此，我萌生了将中英两种文字汇集成册的愿望，并很快得到了清华大学出版社的认可，且最终得以出版。希望此书能够对国内外读者的相互交流发挥作用，让更多的人了解我所从事的艺术教育工作是多么有趣。书中的三十三幅素描作品，都是我在法国和卢森堡驻留期间创作的，它们反映了我在这个时期的艺术创作状态，将它们放在本书的文字间，作为表达自己艺术思想的一个补充吧。

2021 年 3 月于北京

Preface

The words in the book were written by me bit by bit over a long period, among which a few sections were written relatively earlier. The reveries subtly revealed on the pages are closely related to my own experiences in art education, therefore the book was named "Reveries". It is crucial to meditate on teaching and artistic creation, but it is also essential to write it out — meditation without being recorded is meaningless. However, there is another interesting reason for the publication of this book. Claire, the translator of the manuscript, is an old friend of mine who has lived in France for a long time. With a strong passion for art and a profound study of Chinese culture, she has a good understanding of my creative ideas and teaching styles in art. She read the words I wrote very carefully and has made strenuous efforts in translating some of them into English. I have always admired her character and talents, inspiring me to combine the Chinese and English versions into one book. The idea was soon approved by Tsinghua University Press, which made this book's publication possible. I hope this book can play a role in the mutual communication between readers at home and abroad, letting more people understand how interesting my education work on art is. The 32 sketches in the book were created during my residency in France and Luxembourg, illustrating my state of artistic creation during that period. They were blended in between the lines of the book, serving as a supplement to my artistic thoughts.

March 2021, Beijing

Translator's Words

It is an honour to have been asked by Professor Li to translate his book and it is with great pleasure that I accept his request to present the artist and the teacher to his readers worldwide. I met Li Mu on his first sabbatical abroad at the International Arts Centre in Paris in 1996. At that time he was a lecturer at the Central School of Art and Design in Beijing, now amalgamated with Tsinghua University. Since then we have collaborated in promoting Chinese-European understanding via the organisation of exhibitions of his and his colleagues' work in France and through projects and discussions concerning the arts and beyond—on topics as varied as food traditions and folk art.

From the foundations set by his teachers, notably Wu Guanzhong, Li Mu's work has developed constantly, incorporating elements and influences from his travels in Europe, North Africa and the USA, while his reflexions on art education and the philosophy of creativity have benefitted many generations of students from all over China. Now with this bilingual edition of his writings on art, its pedagogy and its social reach, his ideas will be more readily accessible to an international audience of learners, teachers and amateurs in the field of the creative arts.

Clare Perkins Cleret

Authon du Perche, France

July 2020

目　　录（Contents）

艺术不需要"懂你"

　　这个世界上有一件事是不需要"懂"的，这件事就是"艺术"。"懂"艺术的骄傲和"不懂"艺术的沮丧同样没有价值，因为艺术需要的是"感悟"，用全部的身心去感悟，而不是理性分析。艺术不是用法则、规律、定义构成的，因此也就不能用这样的方式去解析。你越是想读懂艺术，它就越是与你相去甚远；反之则会离你越近。艺术就像一种美丽的病毒一样，永远追随并且感染那些不依靠规则去解读它的"冒傻气的人"。我们从艺术中获得的往往不是知识和经验，我们获得的是震撼、冲击和感动。曾有多少人在"懂得"艺术的状态下妄自尊大，又有多少人在"不懂得"艺术的情形下妄自菲薄。现在所有的这些都不重要了，重要的是我们的灵魂与肉体是否还有所感觉，感觉得越多，获得的也就越多。类似的事情在这世界上还有一件，那就是——爱情。

Art Doesn't Demand Comprehension

If there is one thing in this world that doesn't need "comprehension", then that thing is "art". The pride people feel in "comprehending" art and the shame people feel in "not comprehending" art are both equally irrelevant, because what is needed for art is empathy, using one's whole being, both physically and emotionally, to react to art rather than using reason and logic. Art is not structured from rules, regulations and definitions, nor does art use them to provide answers. The more one tries to understand art, the more fundamentally strange it becomes, while oddly, at the same time, it seems to come closer. So really, art resembles a beautiful virus chasing and infecting those who are "soft in the head" and who do not depend on rules to understand it. What often comes to us from art is not knowledge or experience; what we receive is shock, impact and emotion. How many people are there who, considering that they "comprehend" art, are pretentious, and how many are there who think they "don't comprehend" and feel ashamed of themselves. Actually, all these things are of no importance; the important thing is whether or not the mind and body feel some kind of emotion, a real emotion and that they become more and more conscious of that emotion. Actually there is another similar example of this type of sensation—it's called love.

体验涂抹的快乐

绘画本来就具有涂抹之意，只是随着时代的改变，它原先的职能与作用都发生变化而已。如今的绘画已经是高度技术化、职业化、商业化体系下的产物或者产品，我们已经很难想象绘画本身曾经具有的随意、天然、自如的可贵品质，也很难知道绘画的上述性质曾经，而且还将对人类发挥的巨大影响力。我们今天与绘画的关系完全不是人与艺术之间的关系，倒像是人与商业产品间利用与被利用的关系。如果说以往的绘画所具有的那些"朴素品质"是由当时特定的历史条件所决定的话，那么在当今现实主义社会中重新审视何为"朴素"时，我们更有理由去重新追寻和体验那些品质所拥有的快乐。因为我们大家都越来越不快乐！

重温涂抹的随意，因为绘画本来就不是一种专门的技能。寻找涂抹的乐趣，因为涂抹本身不需要任何规则作为依据。体验涂抹的刺激，因为只有通过刺激，才能唤醒我们本性之中最真诚、最善良、最美好的诉求。这个诉求就是：每个人不受束缚、不被干扰地享有独立与自主。

The Joy of Spreading Paint

Basically painting means spreading paint around, but its primary functions and uses adapt to the times. Today's painting has become the result or product of sophisticated technical, professional and commercial development, and we now find it difficult to imagine the voluntary, natural and spontaneous worth of painting itself; it is also difficult to know what the painting that embodied such characteristics meant to human beings, or what enormous influence it could have on humanity. Our relationship with painting today is not at all the same as the relationship between people and art; it's like the relationship between people and the utilization and exploitation of commercial products. If we say the "primitive qualities" of painting of previous centuries are determined by the specific historical conditions, then in that case, when looking afresh at the "primitives" in this realist society at present, we have all the more reason to seek and experience the enjoyment provided by those qualities, because we all seem to be enjoying life less and less!

We should reconsider spontaneity when applying paint, because fundamentally painting is not a specialist skill. We should find the fun in applying paint, because in fact daubing doesn't require observance of any particular rules. We can experience the excitement of spreading paint, because only through stimulation can we inspire the quest for the sincerest, the most benevolent and the most beautiful facets of our nature. This search is aimed at ensuring that no one should suffer constraint or disturbance, at safeguarding their independence and autonomy.

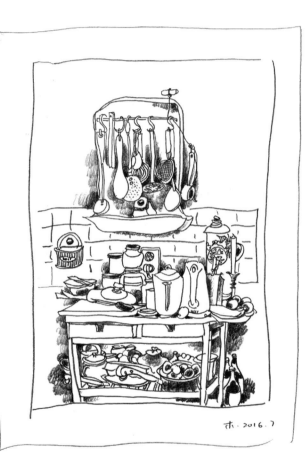

木·2016.7

两种智慧

看印度瑜伽大师艾扬格所著《光耀生命》一书，感想太多。书中提到人类的智慧分为两种，一种是"辨识之智"，另一种是"灵性之智"，而我们现在缺少的恰恰是灵性。我很认同艾扬格的说法，其实这一主题以往我在教学和文字中也多有涉及，只是不够透彻和精辟罢了。所谓的"辨识之智"是指用科学的、经验的、理性的方式认识事物，而"灵性之智"则是运用人类自身的潜能、本性、知觉去感受事物。这两种智慧间的关系往往是此消彼长，"灵性之窗"只有在"辨识之门"完全关闭时才会彻底打开；而每当我们面对开启的"灵性之窗"时，那种震撼和超越之感就会应运而生，关于这一观点我们可以从创作和欣赏艺术的过程中得到印证。"灵性之智"的开启不但有益于我们的身心完善，也有益于"辨识之智"的认知和发展；对于灵性的漠视则必然会导致辨识本身的僵化和衰亡。我们可以通过学习和生活获得许多的辨识本领，但也别忘了我们身上的灵性力量是与生俱来的，不能顾此失彼。我愿意相信天空是由空气、水分等元素所组成的，但我更愿意相信天空既是五彩缤纷的，也是湛蓝的……

Two Kinds of Awareness

When I read *Light on Life*, written by the Indian Yoga Master B. K. S. Iyengar, it gave me a lot to think about because in the book he talks about two types of human awareness. One sort of awareness is acquired through analysis; the other via a spiritual approach. And precisely what is lacking at the present time is spirituality. I can clearly identify with what Iyengar writes: in fact, in my teaching and writing activities this subject has long been one of my latent concerns, although I never really looked into it attentively. On the one hand, what we understand by analytical awareness is the knowledge of things acquired in a scientific, experimental and logical manner. On the other hand, what we call spiritual awareness is the feeling for things arising from the inborn energy, instinct and perception of the individual human being. The relationship between these two kinds of awareness is one of relative ebb and flow: the window towards the spiritual can only be fully open when the door to the analytical has been firmly closed. So looking through the spiritual window presents an opportunity to surprise and excel; one only has to look at how art is created and appreciated to know that this is true. Not only is the opening up of spiritual awareness beneficial to our physical and emotional wellbeing, it also improves our knowledge and the development of our analytical awareness; disregard for the benefits of the spiritual will inevitably lead to the sclerosis and decline of the analytical. Through study and life experience one can build up a huge capacity for analytical knowledge, but we should not forget that each person's spiritual strength is a part of a full and complete life and that we ought to keep them balance. I'd like to believe that the sky is made up of air, vapour and various other elements, but I want to believe even more strongly that while it is made up of all the colours of the rainbow, it is also deep blue...

冻. 2016.7.

艺术没有那么坚硬

艺术从来都不是绝对"坚硬的"，也不是与之对立的绝对"软弱"。我们习惯于艺术的肯定性，习惯于艺术的明确性，也习惯于艺术的表达性，甚至艺术的说教性。但是我们似乎忘了艺术所应具有的不确定性、矛盾性、复杂性以及它纠结和柔弱的另一面。表达"稳固"是一种美，表达"流动"也是另一种美。就像男性之美无法与女性之美相提并论一样，多年的艺术说教，歪曲了我们对"艺术正负两极"中所谓正面效应的理解，似乎正面的意义只能包含在加强、完备、宏大、有力、坚韧以及粗犷之中；而处于事物相反一面的那些因素诸如柔弱、怀疑、恐惧、胆怯、细致等，则受到长期的鄙视。

其实无论是男女之间的"性别之美"，还是正负之间的"性质之美"，人性辉煌的最终显现才是它们的光芒所在。脱离了这个关键环节绝对化地去认识"艺术之美"的做法本身就是丑恶的。因为我们在感受到阳刚之美的同时也能看到阳刚的残暴，在体验到阴柔之美的同时也能看到阴柔的歹毒。生活之美的价值就在于它的双重性及其多重意义，阳刚未必缺少阴柔，阴柔未必缺乏阳刚，"刚柔并举""正负交融"才是正理，相比之下所谓"艺术之美"是否显得过于简单和粗糙呢？

古今中外所有杰出艺术家和艺术作品的存在意义都不是单向性的：凡·高的脆弱导致了他"疯狂"；

贝多芬的强大来自于他的"卑微";阿炳的永恒源于他的自我怜悯。没有任何一个真诚的艺术家会感到自己强大,强大到失去自我怀疑的宝贵能力。他们永远活在忐忑不安之中,永远活在浑浑噩噩之中,也永远活在我们心目中。

木.2016.7.

Art Is Not Set in Stone

Art is never absolutely "rigidly set", neither is it the opposite: "completely malleable". We are accustomed to art being affirmative, explicit, expressive and even informative. But we seem to forget that it has essential qualities of uncertainty, contradiction and complication, as well as a hesitant and delicate side. Expressing "solidity" is one aesthetic, and expressing "fluidity" is another. So just as masculine beauty and feminine beauty cannot be considered on the same footing, many years of people being told what to think about art have provided confused notions of the "opposite poles in art" — clear meaning can only be delivered through reinforcement, completion, enlargement, force, complementarity and vulgarity; factors such as gentleness, doubt, anxiety, uncertainty and refinement that inhabit the other side of the picture are merely ignored with disdain.

In reality, whether we consider "gender beauty" as in masculine and feminine or "elemental beauty" as in positive and negative, in the end, only the radiance of human nature is discernible where it casts its light. Ignoring these crucial dualities in order to acquire the know-how of "art beauty" basically stinks. Because as one is sensitive to "yang" or masculine beauty, he can also perceive its brutal side; when one experiences "yin" or feminine beauty, he may also be aware of its nefarious quality. The value of beauty in life resides in its binary nature and its enormous significance: the masculine or "yang" side is not necessarily lacking something of the feminine or "yin"; the feminine or "yin" is not necessarily missing something of the "yang" or masculine. If the concepts of "simultaneous development of harsh and gentle" and "interconnection of poles" are merely reasoning, then comparatively isn't the notion of "art beauty" too simple and basic?

The significance of all the outstanding artists and their works at home and abroad is not at all monodirectional. Van Gogh's sensitivity led to his "madness"; Beethoven's greatness resides in his "humility"; the famous blind Chinese musician A Bing's enduring notoriety lies in his self-deprecation. There is no one single honest artist who is willing to recognise his own greatness, which would lead to the lost of the precious capacity of self-doubtness. Their existence was in perpetual anxiety and discomfort; they are forever alive in our minds.

塞·托姆布雷

几经辗转，好不容易委托身在广州的得意门生从境外购得美国艺术家塞·托姆布雷的画册，欣喜之余撕开包装，一口气翻阅下去，真是不出所料地让自己再一次赞叹不已：在雪白的画布上用一支支铅笔"不假思索"地"一口气"信手涂鸦下去，线条在颜料的上面翻滚穿梭，颜料在线条之间任意流淌。既像儿童在"掩饰稚嫩"，又像老头在"卖弄天真"，一老一少你来我往好不让人羡慕，几乎让人热泪盈眶，真是好极了。其实老塞在国际上的地位早有公论，他为当代文化所做的贡献可以算得上是卓越的。有关这一点，可以通过最近英国泰特现代美术馆为这位出生于意大利的艺术家所举办的二十年回顾展，以及他应邀为卢浮宫创作永久性艺术作品《艺术眼》得以证明——如果我们还需要通过这样的方式去证明的话。

说到"证明"，令人遗憾的是，到 2019 年的今天为止，我们很少见到对于塞·托姆布雷艺术的介绍，即便是在专业的美术院校，也很少有人了解他以及他所做出的杰出贡献，甚至买不到他的作品选集。我们经常标榜要学习甚至超越先进的文化，但我们只认识艺术的"相同"，不接纳艺术的"不同"，以至于用"相同"去屏蔽"不同"。我们在艺术上太偏激、太单调、太傲慢，也太无知了。我们原本不应该是这个样子的，我们曾经有过那么灿烂的艺术和文化，就是因为我们对待不同的文化和艺术从来都是宽容的。

Cy Twombly[1]

By delegating a challenging task to a star student of mine in Guangzhou, I eventually manage to obtain by this roundabout route a book on Cy Twombly and his paintings form distant abroad. When it arrives, I can't wait to tear off the wrapping and start leafing through it straightaway. As expected I allow myself the endless repetition of this pleasure. On the snow-white canvas, freehand scribbling uses "instinctive" and "immediate" pencil strokes, lines are breaking in successive waves on coloured surfaces, colours are pouring spontaneously into the spaces between the lines. With both a childlike "denial of ingenuousness" and the "innocent frankness" that age can display, this reciprocated duality in Twombly's painting can only elicit huge admiration—his work is wonderful to the point of being deeply moving. Of course, Twombly already had a well-established international reputation, with his contribution to contemporary culture already greatly valued. On this point, one can refer to his 2008 retrospective organised at the Tate Modern in London, and the recognition displayed by the invitation to create a permanent work *Art Eye* for the Louvre—if we still have to use this kind of reference as recognition!

Speaking of "recognition", it is regrettable that even in 2019 we see very little about Cy Twombly. Even in our specialist

---

1　CY Twombly,born Edwin Parker Twombly 1928 Lexington, Virginia, USA; died Rome 2011 art schools, very few people understand him and his extraordinary contribution, to the extent that there is so little demand for books of his works that most bookshops do not bother to stock them. We often say that through study we intend to surpass present and contemporary culture, but we only seem to venture among the "similar", and do not become part of the "dissimilar", even to the extent of using the "similar" in place of the "dissimilar". Concerning art, we may be too extreme, too monotonous, too arrogant or too ignorant. But really, we shouldn't have to be like this. We have a brilliant artistic and cultural past, because we have always integrated different forms of culture and art into our own.

艺术是平面的

在儿童的眼中，从来就没有什么"立体""透视"以及"空间"等成人头脑中的这些概念。有的只是色彩，有的只是形状，有的只是他们使用这些色彩和形状的天性与本能。所以在儿童的心目中，艺术与生活是一体的，是一回事。

成人之所以无法长久地保持这种天性和本能，是因为获得了太多的知识和经验，并且依靠这些知识和经验进行理性的分析，处理他们与生活之间的关系。所以在大多数成人的心目中艺术与生活是分离的，是两回事。他们的眼中也不可能有太多的颜色和形态，也不可能有太多的天性和本能；有的只是各种各样的知识与概念，或者说是别人传授的知识和概念。知识越多，规则越多；概念越多，成见越多；规则和成见越多，作为承载和调和我们与生活之间关系的艺术就越少。而一个缺少艺术的社会就如同一个没有儿童的社会一样不可救药，因为天真是一个家庭、一个社会存在与和谐的基础。

作为艺术教育基础训练的一个环节，平面化的色彩表现方法虽然不能等同于艺术的标准和儿童绘画，却具有艺术和儿童所具有的质朴和天真，具有简化生活、归纳生活，简化事物、归纳事物之功效。因为学会辨别、判断、处理复杂事物的能力是所有学习艺术的人都必须具有的。

Art Is Flat

In the eyes of a child, there are none of those concepts of "three dimensional", "perspective" or "space" which are constructs of the adult mind. For children, there are just colours, shapes, and their nature or mood of using colours and shapes. So, in the mind's eye of the child, art and life are one and the same.

The reason for adults' inability to maintain such attitudes and moods over time is that they have acquired too much knowledge and experience. On the strength of this they make rational decisions and create links between themselves and their lives, so that in the mind-set of many adults, art and life are completely separate entities concerning two completely different matters. They cannot perceive so many colours and forms, or have awareness of so many attitudes and moods. People have various bits of knowledge and certain attitudes that they have picked up or have been passed down to them. The more knowledge there is, the more rules there are. The more concepts there are, the more prejudice there is. The more rules and prejudices there are, the less art is produced that can help us to deal with our lives; and a society without art is as incurable as a society without children, because innocence is the foundation stone for the existence of, and harmony within, families and societies.

As a part of the basic training in art education, flattened colour as a means of expression—although not the same thing as formal art and children's painting—can retain a natural quality and innocence found in both art and children; it simplifies and summarizes life, simplifies subjects and simplifies the effect of things. Because acquiring the competence to discuss, judge and organize the complexity of things is absolutely essential for all students of art.

他们和我们

他们在画，我们在看。他们在说，我们在听。我们在"有目的"地看和听，他们在"无目的"地画和说。他们不是在为我们画，我们却是在为他们看。他们更善于在画中说，我们却不善于在画中听。

绘画是他们的母语，与其说他们是在听、说、读、写，不如说他们是在唱、念、做、打。是才能，更是天性。不是每个人都有才能，却是每个人都有天性。才能是片面的，天性是普遍的。才能可以受到文明的抑制，天性却能启迪文明。以往我们只知眷顾绘画中的才能，如今开始瞩目绘画中的天性。才能属于艺术，天性属于生活。没有"目的"，没有"意义"，没有"企图"，不知道他们还会画什么，只知道他们在不断地画：画鲜艳与不鲜艳，画狂放与再狂放，画天真与更天真。不确定这到底是他们的艺术，还是他们的生活。人们都说艺术源于生活且高于生活，在此他们的艺术等同于生活。

如果说他们是一群来自遥远"自闭"天地中的天真者，他们正在用"绘话"的天性对我们诉说，那么我们不该聆听并且回应他们吗？

Them and Us

They are painting; we are watching. They are talking; we are listening. We are watching and listening "with a purpose". They are painting and talking "without a purpose". They are not aiming their painting at us, but we are looking at them. They are better at talking through painting than we are at listening to painting.

Painting is their mother tongue; though one could say they sing, recite, compose and play rather than listening, speaking, reading and writing. They have ability; one could even say it is in their nature. It's not that everyone has ability; it is rather that everyone has his or her nature. Ability is individual while nature is universal. Ability may be subject to the restraints of culture, whereas inborn nature can inspire culture. In the past, we were only concerned with ability in painting; now we are looking more closely to distinguish the nature as expressed in painting. Ability is part of art whereas the nature is part of life. When there is no "purpose" or "meaning" or "striving", we don't know what else they are going to paint; we just know that they will never stop painting. It may be fresh and inventive or not. It may be unhindered or become even more unhindered. It may be naïve or even more naïve. It is not clear whether this is their art or their life. Everyone is ready to say that art springs from life and blossoms in life: in this respect, their art is on the same footing as life.

And if we say that they are a group of innocents from a distant "locked in" world, and that they communicate with us through their "paint speak" nature, should we not to listen respectfully to what they are saying so that we are able to respond?

木. 2016. 8.

油画是个老家伙

油画这玩意儿传入中国也有一百多年了，虽然比起它的西洋祖宗来说，我们的油画还很年轻，但在"心理年龄"上却远比它的长辈们老成。如果说我们的油画远离了它那"初生牛犊不怕虎"的时代，那么依据正常的发展演变步伐，在西方前辈们不间断地锐意进取、推陈出新的作为面前，中国油画则显现出了掩饰不住的顽固和年迈。

在油画艺术的故乡，前辈们曾经透过油画这面镜子审视思想意识的改变，通过油画这个手段去经历从职业化到大众化的蜕变，经由油画这个窗口去反思生活的意义和生存的价值。而在油画艺术的他乡，我们自己的艺术并没有因为油画的到来而获得拯救和新生，反而丧失了原有的品质和特点。

油画和中国画的关系就像油和水一样永远不能调和。我们的油画曾经作为意识形态的工具，我们的油画正在逐渐地成为一个产业、一种行业，成为越来越多的人发财致富的源泉，它已经变得越来越与我们的生活无关。也许我们在一个世纪以前引进的并不是西方艺术的根本，而仅仅是获取了一个绘画的品种、一种特殊的技艺。也许我们当初看上的只是油画华丽的外表，而没有在意潜藏在这个美丽外表之下的那颗活跃和不安分的心灵，没有意识到油画艺术的发展演变实际上连带着西方现代思想文化的发展和演变。

我们恐怕无论如何都无法确定，当初引进油画这个玩意儿对于我们自己的文化艺术来说到底是幸运还是灾难。至少到目前为止，我们还没有充足的理由可以庆幸、可以乐观。

Our Old Friend—Oil Painting

Although the oil painting arrived in China over a century ago, Chinese oil painting is still young in comparison to its Western predecessors but mentally it is more mature and thoughtful. If a comparison is made in terms of "physiology", Chinese oil painting has already outgrown its "new-born calf fears no tiger" period; if we consider a normal pace of development to be similar to that displayed by the Western elders' uninterrupted determined progression, where new talent abandons the old ways to seek constant innovation, then contemporary Chinese painters seem stuck in their ways.

In the homeland of the art of oil painting, Western artists examined changes in their thoughts and ideas through the lens of oil painting; they experienced the metamorphosis from industrialization to popularization through the actions of painting; they perceived the value and significance of life and existence through the window of oil painting. However, in the new environment that included the art of oil painting, our own art did not thrive and undergo a renaissance; on the contrary, it lost its quality and specificity.

The relationship between oil painting and Chinese painting is the same as that between oil and water —they just don't blend. In the past, our oil painting was a means to give shape to an idea. Now our oil painting is becoming a production line, an industry and a fountain of fortune for an increasing number of people; it is becoming more and more irrelevant to our lives. Maybe what we introduced a century ago wasn't the fundamental of Western art at all, but simply a way to paint, a particular sort of draughtsmanship. Perhaps what we initially perceive is only the smooth facade of oil painting, without seriously considering the restless and animated spirit behind the beautiful canvas curtain. Perhaps we lack an awareness of the relationship between the development of oil painting and the development of contemporary Western attitudes to culture.

In any event, we may wonder if it is possible to know whether introducing the oil painting was auspicious or calamitous for our own art and culture. The least we can say is that for the time being we still don't really have sufficient motivation for optimistic rejoicing.

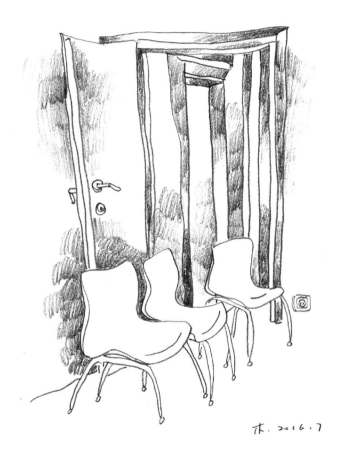

木. 2016.7

奥赛的意义

对于多数国人来说，位于巴黎塞纳河畔、集中展示19世纪后期至20世纪初近代艺术的奥赛美术馆，比起其他美术馆有着更加特殊的意义，因为这里的艺术与我们的信念、文化、审美、情感息息相关。相对于罗浮宫的宗教情怀、蓬皮杜的现代意识，我们似乎更愿意重温那些伴随着理想、记忆与激情的浪漫主义、现实主义、印象主义的艺术作品。更何况那些伟大的艺术家作品的光芒，几近代表着我们对于艺术的全部理解和信仰。

从多年的闭关锁国、对自己传统的否定，到后来的改革开放、选择性地借鉴西方，我们缔造了一个复杂、矛盾、独一无二的"审美判断文化"，这个文化的取向是关于崇高、自主、唯美和叛逆的。它既独立又依从，既浪漫又现实，既崇高又肤浅，既矜持又疯狂。这是社会文明进程的一个重要组成部分，我们的生活就是在这样的文化中存在着，它将支配我们很长的时间。我们喜爱罗丹的抒情，伴随着对巴尔扎克的认同；我们崇尚莫奈的色彩，夹杂着对自由的向往；我们痴迷于凡·高的苦难，浸透着每个人同样的生活体验。就像我们沉浸在肖邦、贝多芬、柴可夫斯基、披头士的音乐中，完成"自我的启蒙"一样，艺术的重要在于公众，在于公众的被唤醒。多少国内艺术家在"奥赛"的那些雕像前泪流满面，这是他们曾经的精神家园，他们回来了。多少国人在"奥赛"的绘画前驻足流连，这是他们久违的精神盛宴，他们如愿了。一个世纪以来我们国家、社会、个体的文化变迁，十分生动和形象地在"奥赛"的艺术时空中显现出来；我们的过去、现在或许还有未来的精神寄托，还会处在它那美好、平和、丰富的显现之中。也许当初的创建者们不曾想到，这所博物馆对于占世界人口五分之一的中华大国来说究竟意味着什么。在中国访客面前，"奥赛"不是梦，它是梦的实现。

　　我曾带着自己的那份敬仰，几度走访这座众人心目中的艺术殿堂。建筑、雕塑、绘画等空间的艺术，却随着思绪在时间中流淌。偌大的一个展场任由美的事物到处摆放，引诱我采摘和品尝。从前的火车站站台已变为展览大厅，画里画外、楼上楼下，真实与虚拟的人们相互张望。罗丹的《地狱之门》《巴尔扎克雕像》，早已为我们熟知；米勒的《牧羊女》、库尔贝的《画室》，我们曾长久向往；莱尔米特的《收割后的报酬》曾在1979年随"十九世纪法国农村风景画"展来北京展出，给很多人留下难以磨灭的印象。最让人魂牵梦萦的要数马奈、莫奈，还有塞尚、凡·高、高更、雷诺阿等人的作品；著名的《草地午餐》《阳光灿烂中的鲁昂教堂》《玩纸牌者》《向日葵》《白马》《煎饼磨坊的舞会》等未曾相见的老朋友，在这儿都能看到。奥赛美术馆印象派和后印象派作品收藏之多、之全、之美，超越我的想象。抽离了古代艺术的虔诚，去除了当代艺术的紧张，只是在塑造和触摸的体验中与艺术互论短长。伟大与普通不再有区别，创造与欣赏不再有不同，交流成为交融，观看化为想象。凝视的目光、呆滞的表情、放松的心境；艺术家、艺术作品、艺术欣赏，谁更重要呢？

令人不可思议的是，这样一个承载量巨大的博物馆，从落成至今不过短短二十六年，在拥有众多博物馆的法国无疑是年轻的。古老车站建筑的前身，系统完整的作品收藏，政府不遗余力的投入，都是成就它今日辉煌的前提保障。作为一个专业美术馆，它所呈现的不光是艺术作品，还有艺术生成的原因，以及艺术带给人们的幻想和希望。

More than Just a Place for Art

For many of us Chinese, the Orsay Museum, situated on the left bank of the Seine in Paris exhibiting art collections from the second half of the 19th to the early years of the 20th century, has a special significance, as both greater than and different to other museums, because here the art seems so closely connected to our beliefs, culture, aesthetics and emotions—so infused with the same breath. Compared to the religious art in the Louvre or the contemporary awareness in the Pompidou Centre, we somehow prefer to contemplate Orsay's romantic, realist and impressionist works that reflect ideals, memories and enthusiasms. And what's more, the radiance of these fabulous works by great artists seems ready to illuminate all our understanding and beliefs regarding art.

After many years of closed doors and isolation, rejection of our own traditions, followed by a period of outward orientated reforms and a time of learning selectively from the West, we have created a uniquely contradictory and confused culture of aesthetic judgement which is moving in directions of the sublime, the autonomous, the beautiful and the provocative. It is both individualistic and conformist, both romantic and realist, both detached and oppressive, both reserved and frenzied. This is a very important part of the development process of a society's shared civilisation and our life actually happens within this model of civilisation, affecting us for years to come. We love Rodin's creative expression in his statue of Balzac, so we identify with the author. We advocate Monet's use of colour, confusing it with aspirations towards liberty. We are fascinated by Van Gogh's suffering, so we transfuse it into every similar personal experience. Likewise, when we immerse ourselves in the music of Chopin, Beethoven, Tchaikovsky or the Beatles and attain a state of "self-enlightenment", the importance of the art is to be found in the reaction of the audience, in the stimulating effect it has on them. How many Chinese artists, standing before those Orsay statues, with tears running down their cheeks, realise they have returned to their soul's native heath? How many Chinese travellers, mesmerised by the Orsay paintings, realise this is the long awaited spiritual banquet and that their wish has come true? The upheavals in national, social and individual culture of the past hundred years come to life in a dynamic and evocative way in the spatial and temporal elements of "Orsay" art; our past and present can look to the future in the spiritual heaven existing in the midst of the beauty, tranquillity and richness of the museum. At the start, the founders probably never imagined what this museum could really mean to the Chinese (who constitute a fifth of the world's population) or that in Chinese art lovers' eyes, "Orsay" is not a dream, the Orsay Museum is a dream come true.

Personally, I have the deepest respect for the Orsay Museum and I have often visited this widely appreciated palace of art. Here architecture, sculpture, painting and other spatial arts follow thought processes that run through time; the extent of the vast gallery responsible for showing countless beautiful exhibits has led me to select and savour certain examples. The old station platforms have been transformed to a huge exhibition hall, where from within the paintings and outside the frames, from above or below, the real and imaginary characters gaze at each other. We all know as old friends Rodin's *Gates of Hell* and his *Monument to Balzac*, just as we have also admired Millet's *Shepherdess with her Flock* and Courbet's *Artist's Studio*. Leon-Auguste Lhermitte's *Paying the Harvesters* was part of the "19th

Century French Rural Landscape Painting" exhibition in Beijing in 1979 that left an indelible impression on so many minds. Among the artists whose works are also unforgettable are Manet and Monet, also Cezanne, van Gogh, Gaughin and Renoir and their celebrated *Dé-jeuner sur l'Herbe, Rouen Cathedral, Full Sunlight, The Card Players, Sunflowers, White Horse, Dance at the Moulin de la Galette,* who were old friends from reproductions in books but who we had never met face to face. The quantity, the extent and the beauty of the Orsay collection of Impressionists and Post-Impressionists exceeded anything I could imagine. It is only when the devotional aspect of early art is abstracted and when the tensions of contemporary works have been put aside that the observation of form and use of materials can lead to proper discussion on artistic scope. The grandiose and the ordinary as subjects no longer present any differences, creativeness and appreciation cease to be dissimilar, exchanging becomes blending, while contemplation morphs into imagination. Tranquil perception, the expression of stillness, the mind-set of "letting go"; artists, art works, art appreciation: we can ponder on their relative importance.

It is difficult for most people to imagine that, in a country like France, which is full of museums, the inauguration of this immense and extensive exhibition space took place as recently as 1986. The old façade of the converted station, the complete and systematic representation of the collections, the strong and continued official support are all solid guarantees for the continued achievement and renown of the museum. Now established as a specialist art gallery, what it respectfully presents to the public is not only works of art, but also a setting for the creativeness with both vision and hope that art offers to its audience.

木. 2016. 7.

清华园中的启蒙

能够通过绘画的方式了解自己的母校，恐怕是美术学院学生一生中最重要的机遇和幸运，这也成为清华大学美术学院区别于其他院校的一个重要艺术教学特点，因为清华园有着太多的它对我们和我们对它的非凡承载。艺术意味着什么，清华意味着什么，我们自己意味着什么，需要每一位学生在校园的写生过程中，自己去寻求独立、自由的答案。

当写生的目的不再是客观的记录、不再是技巧的展现，而是我们面对客观事物所做出的一项属于我们自己的判断和选择的时候，学生们的人生意义才算是真正地形成了，他们作品的艺术价值才算是真正地实现了。选择什么、描绘什么、怎样描绘，面对偌大的清华校园，写生者的艺术素养和创新能力将接受前所未有的审视和挑战。

通常在我们描述对于事物的认知时，往往会不由自主地带有既往的习惯与经验；然而艺术创作的特殊性则要求创作者排除"偏见"去寻找新的描述方式，并且从这种描述中获得新的经验与习惯，或者说是新的认知。我们对于未来的"清华园"的期待，应该从对它全新的认知开始，因为这样的认知，必将导致一个个"崭新的未来"的显现。

一届又一届的学生走进、走出清华的校园，他们带来的是幻想、敬仰和经验，他们带走的是探索、发现和思想。一幅幅校园写生作品既描绘了清华园的历史变迁，又揭示了描绘者的心灵变迁，他们都变得不同于以往。清华园留给了他们不同的思索痕迹，他们每个人心目中的清华是不同的，他们每个人的思想也是不同的。

Starting at Tsinghua

Being able to understand your own school from ways of painting may be the very best thing that can ever happen to an art student: this teaching methods at the Art School of Tsinghua differ greatly with other art schools. This is because Tsinghua University plays an important role in the relationship between the institution itself and our art department. The significance of art, the significance of Tsinghua, one's own significance—whenever students pick up a pen or a paintbrush in class, they are all seeking personal responses to questions about independence and individuality.

The aim of drawing is not to make an objective record or a show of skill, but to describe the feelings experienced when faced with an objective thing. They belong to the moment of our decisions and choices, allowing the significance of a student's life to take shape authentically, allowing the true artistic value of the students' work to emerge. Selecting something, sketching something, how you draw something, in the context of such a prestigious institution as Tsinghua: the potential training and innovation of future artists depend on the integration of unprecedented judgment and debate.

Generally, when we become aware of how we are portraying the subject of our work, without realizing it, we tend to bring in old habits and previous experience; consequently individual creativity requires the artist to avoid any "bias" by seeking a new graphic style and, from personal innovative description, acquire new experience and establish new habits, in other words, create a new awareness. Concerning the future prospects of Tsinghua, we should immediately be conscious of each instance of completely fresh awareness, and as soon as it appears, we should accept and greet each example of a "brand new future" in turn.

With each new intake at Tsinghua, the students bring us their imagination, their hopes and their experience; with each graduation, they take away with them their discoveries, concepts and ideas. Every piece of student artwork produced at the school illustrates the development of Tsinghua's history and inspires the understanding of changes in the artists' outlook, always differing from past examples. Tsinghua provides each of them with different thinking processes; every one of them sees a different Tsinghua in their mind's eye; each of them has different ideas.

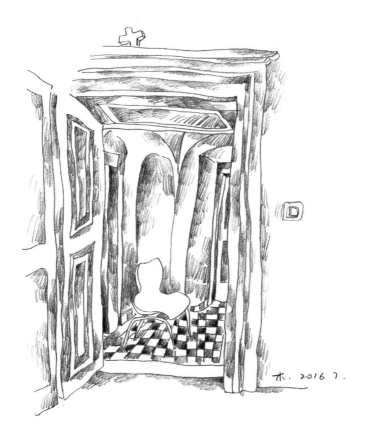

山楂树下的教师们

车窗外的景色吻合着《山楂树》的歌声轻快闪过。这首萦绕了几代人的老歌，总是在人们需要它的时候显现出新鲜的面容，以至于每次听到它的时候，都会渗透进你的思绪，让你在快乐、苦恼、兴奋、失落的混合体验中，反复品尝失去和获得的滋味。它既脆弱又坚强，既快乐又忧伤，既清晰又迷茫。此时我想不起别的人，除了刚刚结束的美术教师进修班的教师们。

不知是什么原因，每当我遇见在中学执教的美术教师，心里总是有几分酸楚。也许因为自己是教师，知道教师的艰辛，并且知道这艰辛很大程度上来源于无法言说的苦。所以走进教室之前，我已经有了几分敬畏之情。进修班中年轻老师居多，可我感受不到年龄的差异。大家都那么和颜悦色、文质彬彬，总体来说是拘谨和内敛的。即使在夜晚的聚会上，也很难看到大家真实和自然的一面，所有人都是可尊的、可敬的，但看不出可亲。不知道大家内心深处的热情、童真、特色是否依然留存，也不知道好奇、挑衅、固执是否存在。在相互接触和交流中，这些珍贵的因素都显露不多；即便是在最需要抒发真情实感的绘画作品里，也不太容易看到教师们内心世界的生动表达。也许他们已经尽量去表达了，但表达得含蓄且客观。我努力去感受他们的心灵话语，尽力去体会他们的智慧闪现，感受和体会他们每一个人的独特存在，尽管这种感受和体会来得并不轻松。

北京的经历、清华的氛围、名人的指点，这一切能不能构成我们期待的率真、至善和完美，我不知道。因为我感觉不到与这些因素有关的结果，那就是作为教师的快乐。我们可以忽视很多事情，却不能忽视教师对快乐的追求，因为这很可能是我们所能追求的唯一。生活的意义不是将事物彼此相加就能获得的，而在于激励人们不断地去寻找那些没有"结果"的、没有"目的"的答案，快乐算得上是答案之一。这恐怕也是我们为什么要当教师的原因。教师应该意味着什么：是一个名称、一个工具，还是由具体数字所组成的刺眼的升学率？这些功利的因素与我们一辈子的身心健康和生命意义相比，是否还那么重要？教师的职责是"育人"，可现在最需要"抚育"的，恰恰是我们自己。

在上课的过程中，似乎看到过的每张绘画作业，都有才艺显现之处。在方寸的形色之间，会不经意流露些许趣味、果敢、神秘乃至美妙，有些作品堪称出色，但这些作品好像没有为它们的作者提供应有的自信。虽然所有的教师都出自专业美术院校，有些人甚至曾在令人向往的历史名城圣彼得堡深造，但多数的教师宁愿倾听对他们全画的"规律性"批评，也不愿认同对于他们的"非规律性"赞扬。长期的应试状态几乎摧毁了他们曾经拥有的对于艺术的敏感，尤其是对自己作品中那些稍纵即逝的瞬间的敏感——这是一个艺术家"立命"的底线，也是一个艺术教师"安身"的本钱，一旦丧失，不可逆转。保持艺术的敏感，会倾注我们毕生的精力，但能得到自信且快乐的回报。艺术创作过程中的自信，来自自我"发现"的能力，只有那些有能力"发现"自我的人，才有可能被人"发现"。

也许做教师并非所有人的最终心愿，但很多优秀的艺术作品都是在它们的作者身处"事与愿违"的境遇下产生的，这才是艺术的归宿。教师工作不是职业，而是事业。职业是束缚的，事业是自由的。就像艺术不是职业而是事业一样，将艺术当职业你会倍感痛苦，反之则无比快乐。教授艺术的教师是一类很特殊的人，应该敏锐、自信、快乐、独立，我们应该永远守候在自己的山楂树下，品尝果实的甜酸苦辣。

Under the Hawthorn Tree

Outside the car the landscape flashes past, reminding me of the song "Under the Mountain Hawthorn Tree" (based on a Russian folk tune and one of the few to be heard in the seventies). This signature tune still lingers in the memory and typifies a certain era for many people; it still shows a fresh face whenever people want to hear it, and whenever you listen to it, it gets inside your head and makes you feel a mixture of happiness and sorrow, excitement and disappointment, leaving a complex flavor of both loss and achievement. It is simultaneously fragile and robust, joyful and melancholic, clear and confused. At this moment, I'm not thinking about anyone else but the group of art teachers who have just finished their training course.

I don't know why, but whenever I meet art teachers from middle schools, I always feel pretty sad and aggrieved. Maybe it's because I'm a teacher myself and I'm keenly aware of the problems these teachers face and I know how difficult it is for them to find a way to express the hardships they encounter. So before I go into the classroom, I already feel apprehensive. There are many young teachers in the group, but I didn't realize how wide the age band would be. They are all friendly and cheerful, well-spoken and smart, always reserved and discreet. Even at the evening social event, it is difficult for them to show their real selves and behave in a natural way, so everyone is very sage and respectful but without opening up at all. One cannot tell if they are concealing any heartfelt warm feelings or playful childhood personal imprinting or whether wonderment, provocativeness and perseverance are also

kept under wraps. Even during the time reserved for personal inter-
action and exchange, there is little opportunity for these precious
elements to find expression. Even in their painting, which necessarily requires showing genuine true feelings, it is none too easy to ac-
cess much manifestation of the teachers' inner world. Perhaps they
have gone as far as they can in self-expression, yet what they show
seems to imply the objective rather than anything subjective. I tried
very hard to comprehend what is heartfelt in what they say; I did
my utmost to empathize about where they find their inspiration; I
endeavored to perceive them as individuals even though they find
it difficult to share feelings and experiences.

I don't know whether the experience in Beijing, the am-
biance at Tsinghua and the counsel of reputed academic staff
can all combine to satisfy our expectations of sincerity, good-
ness and perfection. Because I do not feel that the result is to be
found in these particular factors: that would indeed be satisfying
for the teachers. We can neglect many things, but not the teachers' aspiration to wellbeing, because this is very probably our
only important aspiration. The point of our existence is not to
add to our possessions, but to encourage people to constantly
seek the most important outcome—one that provides happiness
rather than achieving "results" or "targets". This may well
be the reason and the motivation to become a teacher. Does the
significance of teaching lie in the role and in the means, or does
it lie in the figures shown by the extraordinary rise in the enrol-
ment rate? Is it still important to make comparisons between
these practical elements and what our generation demonstrates
in the way of physical and mental equilibrium with our modus

vivendi? The duty of teachers is to "educate people" but at the moment what is most necessary is to "tend people", particularly themselves.

During classes, having seen many paintings in my life, they all show some talent. Among the shapes and colors on the canvas, one may be aware of the interest, courage, mystery, even perfection being expressed; there may be some works that have character, but these works probably have not provided their authors with self-confidence. However, all teachers have followed a particular specialist training, some even studied in the prestigious and historic Russian Academy of Arts in St Petersburg. Although many teachers pay attention to a "formalist" critique of their paintings, they do not wish to identify with any "non-formalist" admiration they receive. Years of working for exams may have destroyed their artistic sensitivity, particularly that emotion found in paintings created in an unexpected inspirational moment—this is the base line of the artist's peace of mind and it is also the thread of an art teacher's tranquility; once lost, it is irretrievable. By protecting the inspiration in art, we can preserve the perpetual flow of energy while receiving in return self-confidence and happiness. Self-confidence is gained from the artistic creative process, originating from the potential of "awareness"; it is only the people who are "aware" of their own potential who can lead others to "awareness".

Becoming a teacher may not be everyone's most cherished ambition, but many extraordinary achievements are made in far less favorable conditions than their authors could have wished— just one of the advantages of art. The work of teaching is not a form of business; it's a cause. A business is a form of restraint, a cause is liberation. So in the same way the art is not a business but a cause, by making art into a business, one multiplies the pain instead of increasing the happiness. The art teacher is a particular sort of person, needing to be perspicacious, confident, happy, independent; we must all stay under our own personal hawthorn, savoring all the bittersweet sharpness of its berries.

木. 2016. 7

回忆吴先生教学

吴冠中先生教学，从来不在乎我们是否能准确地描绘事物，也没有传授过什么绘画的技法给我们。他总是先观察，看我们是否已经看懂了我们所要画的对象：无论是风景还是人物，只要你能找到它们各自的特点和规律，并且能够有意识地表达出来，就会受到鼓励，哪怕你的画面还存在着许多技术上的不足。相反，对那些仅仅是客观记录事物的同学作业，吴先生却很不以为然。

记得有一年，吴先生带我们到山东大渔岛写生。按照课程的安排，每天晚上他都会来看同学们的作业，每次都会在部分同学的作业中找到他的兴奋点并且大加评说。而每次受到他表扬的那些画，大多都具有天真、大胆、果断、夸张等特点，其他的画他大概看看也就过去了，不会多说什么。我自己那时候的画儿估计就是属于比较"规矩"的，所以很少引起吴先生的注意，为此我也时常感到苦恼和委屈，也会抱怨老师不够公正。因为他似乎永远对那些我们所认为的"绘画能力"较弱的同学感兴趣，并且对他们那些在当时看来很"幼稚"的画推崇备至。在写生示范过程中，我发现吴先生并没有按照我们眼中看到的"自然规律"去画画，而是按照他自己的"主观规律"在画画。他在课堂上讲的那些现在听来震撼人心的话语，在当时都是不能被接受的，诸如"绘画主要是表现意境""艺术什么都可以没有，但不能没有感情""错觉是艺术之母""形式决定内容"，等等。真正能够理解、领会吴先生的良苦用心，已经是二十年以后的事情了。这些年我不断地画、不断地思考，越来越觉得他当年所说的和所做的一切都是那么正确。如果没有吴先生当年的那些启发、诱导，我不知道自己今天会是什么样子。

在学习艺术的重要阶段能遇上这样的老师，我和我当初的同学们是非常幸运的。而对于今天在美术学院中学习的同学们来说，他们也是幸运的，因为我们正在将吴冠中先生的学术思想贯穿到今天以及今后的教学中去。

Remembering Mr. Wu's Classes

When Wu Guanzhong was teaching, he never paid attention to whether we were drawing objects correctly, nor did he teach us any particular technique. He always observed what we were doing first, to see whether or not we had understood what we were supposed to be drawing—it could be landscape or life drawing—all he wanted us to show was that we had discovered the individual particularities of the subject matter, that we could consciously express them; and then we were given encouragement, even if the technique was still a serious problem. On the other hand, Mr. Wu certainly disapproved of the students' work if it was simply an uninvolved visual record.

I remember one year, Mr. Wu took us to Dayu Island in Shandong Province to do outdoor sketching. The course was organized in a way that every evening he came to look at the students' work and at each session he would pick out elements of certain paintings which inspired his enthusiasm and prompted his critique. Each time he praised a painting, it usually meant that the work had shown a particular freshness, courage, decisiveness or overstatement; for the other paintings, he looked at them and passed on without saying much. I consider my own paintings of that time as belonging to the "conventional" class so they didn't really attract his attention and because of this I felt troubled and in some way the victim of an injustice as if the teacher were not being entirely fair because he always seemed interested in the students whose painting skills we considered not particularly good, while holding in high esteem those we tended to label as childish. For instance, I now realise that Wu Guanzhong was not painting according to our perceived "laws of nature" but according to his own "subjective laws" when he wielded the brush. Now I think of the ground-breaking ideas he was expressing in the classroom, which were unacceptable at the time, such as "the important part of painting is expressing inspiration", "art can lack everything, but not emotion", "illusion is the mother of art", "form determines content" and so on. Nearly twenty years passed before I was able to fully understand and assimilate the convictions of Mr. Wu. During that time, I had painted and pondered constantly, gradually realizing that everything he said and did when he taught was so right. I just don't know what I would have been like today without the inspiration and guidance of Mr. Wu at that time.

My classmates and I were all incredibly lucky to encounter a teacher like Wu Guanzhong at such an important period of our art school studies. And as for the students who are studying in art schools today, they are also very fortunate because we are still passing on Wu Guanzhong's art education ideas in today's teachings and for subsequent use.

作为教师的吴冠中

吴冠中先生是我们国家最杰出的当代艺术家，同时也是当代最杰出的艺术教育家。可以说他对于中国现代艺术发展所做的贡献并不一定比他对于中国现代艺术教育所做的贡献更大。他一生几乎所有关于艺术的创作和努力，都和他的艺术教育经历息息相关，同时也都无可避免地带有他在艺术教育领域奋斗、思索和抗争的烙印与痕迹。

近代中国文化艺术发展、变化的历史，在一定意义上说也是一部有关艺术教育的历史，它十分清晰地反映出近百年来我们在各个历史时期艺术教育观念的变迁与艺术教育方式的改变，而每一次变迁与改变也都预示着艺术观念和方式的变迁和改变。事实上，西方艺术自"进入"中国之日起，与本土艺术在艺术创作与艺术教育方面交相辉映、相互混杂，影响甚至取代的状况就一刻也没有停止过。往往是有什么样的艺术家就会有什么样的艺术教育，有什么样的艺术教育又必然导致有什么样的审美价值观的产生。我们今天审美观的局限应该归咎于同样局限的艺术教育，可造成艺术教育如此局面的，恰恰又是那些在艺术创作上有所局限的艺术家们。中国近代艺术所获得的发展与收获，也可以说就是我国艺术教育本身的发展和收获。中国近代艺术所呈现的扭曲与问题，说到底就是我们艺术教育体制本身的扭曲和问题。

这两者之间的关系太密切了，密切得难分彼此，密切到了它几乎是我们所有艺术教育、艺术创作弊端的根源的地步。

在中国，艺术创作往往也就等于艺术教育，艺术家也理所当然地可以作为艺术教育家或者说教师。他们肩负着创造艺术和教授艺术的双重使命，他们责任重大。然而却很少有人意识到自己同时承担着双重的义务和责任，很少有人愿意或者说能够分清这两类性质完全不同的问题。大多数情况下，这两个问题是被当作同一个问题来对待的；时至今日，这也是我们的艺术教育与世界其他国家艺术教育之间最大的不同。而吴冠中先生则是中国近代艺术教育历史上，为数不多的既承担了义务又尽到了责任的人之一，所以说他是艰难的、出色的、不同寻常的。

作为一名教师，吴冠中先生在艺术教育领域辛勤、艰难、顽强地工作了一辈子，他带给这个艺术教育制度的东西，远远要比他应该从中获得的多得多。年轻时期在国内接受的较为完善的艺术启蒙教育，使他率先体会到艺术创作的感染力及其带给人们生活的巨大改变。后来留学西方的经历使得他有机会能更早地感受到现代艺术理念对于教育的影响，以及对人性的和谐与完善所起到的巨大作用；也使得他在成为教师以后，更快地将他日后逐渐成熟的艺术教育理念实施并推广到他的艺术教育事业中去。这个理念就是：艺术是一项通过视觉因素改变和确立人类审美情感的事业，而不是一项有关技能、法则训练、传授方式的工作。

作为一名艺术家，吴冠中先生深知艺术创作过程的辛苦与艰难，知道这种辛苦与艰难不仅仅来自于对艺术表现方式的追求和掌握，更来自于一个年轻人在试图获得自己所特有的审美与判断能力过程中的痛苦和困惑。他从不提倡学生停留在前人矗立的艺术丰碑面前精益求精，他也从不鼓励学生靠咀嚼他人的残羹剩饭来寻找捷径。他倡导的总是那些发自学生心中的天真想象，那些来自学生眼中的单纯色彩，那些出自学生手中的稚拙图形。他鼓励的永远是那些不抄袭自然，勇敢地创造自我的意境、自我的和谐的人，永远是那些不效法古人、不迷信洋人，开古代、外国的花，结现代、民族的果的人。

作为一个兼有艺术家和教师双重身份的人，吴先生非常清楚艺术创作与艺术教育在思维方式、工作方法上的相同和不同，也清楚作为一名教师该如何引导学生利用好它们的相同、对待好它们的不同。他从不武断地用个人艺术创作的方式代替艺术教育的方法，也从不僵化地以艺术教育的某些法则去阻碍学生们的艺术创作。因为他知道，虽然艺术教育就是教授学生如何进行艺术创作，但不能够以艺术创作的方式来进行，尤其不能够以个人艺术创作的方式来进行。他既呼吁艺术教育所应具有的共性，又提倡艺术创作所应具备的个性。他既提倡在艺术教育过程中需要宽容，又呼吁在艺术创作的过程里需要极端。他既在艺术实践中身先士卒、身体力行，又尽量避免学生因过分地效仿他自己而走入歧途。在近半个多世纪漫长的中国艺术教育历史当中，有多少人接受过吴先生的教诲我们不得而知，但聆听过吴先生指教的学生都或多或少地感觉到他的不同凡响和与众不同。

因为有了作为教师的吴冠中，我们意识到了在绘画的形式和内容之间曾存在着一条难以厘清的界线，并且由此引发了深刻的反思。因为有了作为教师的吴冠中，我们知道了绘画的现代性以及它在我们每个人艺术生命中所起到的重大意义，以至于我们重新认识了塞尚，重新理解了凡·高，并且最终理解认识了他人和自己。因为有了作为教师的吴冠中，我们得以确立属于我们自己的审美价值观，并且将审美教育作为艺术教育的重要环节延续到今后的艺术教育体系中去。因为有了作为教师的吴冠中，艺术教育已不再是艺术创作的附庸，也不再是艺术家个人传授手艺的工具，它已经开始成为一门越来越独立的符合艺术教育科学规律的新兴学科。还是因为有了作为教师的吴冠中，更多受到他艺术教育精神启迪的教师正在认真严肃地思考，如何通过艺术、艺术教育将学生培养成为更加和谐、健全的人，而不是熟练、合格的工具；更多受到他艺术教育精神启发的学生也在严肃认真地思考，如何通过学习艺术使自己具有更加敏锐的判断思考能力、更加独立的审美选择能力。作为艺术家的吴冠中，在艺术创作领域的成就是众所周知、有目共睹的；作为艺术教育家、教师的吴冠中，也同样以他非凡的能力和毅力为国家的艺术教育事业做出巨大的贡献。我们的艺术教育历史中能够有吴冠中这样的教师，是受教育者的幸事，是艺术教育的幸事，是国家的幸事。

Wu Guanzhong as a Teacher

Wu Guanzhong is our country's most celebrated modern artist and is also our most celebrated art educationalist. It is certainly true to say that his contribution to art education was as influential as his contribution to the development of modern art in China. Throughout his life the creativity and energy he devoted to art mirrored his activities in art education while also necessarily bearing the marks of the struggles, reflections and resistance he encountered in the domain of pedagogy.

The history of the developments and the transformations in contemporary art and culture in China is in some sense related to the history of art education; it clearly resonates with the problems arising from the various concepts of art education in each period and the reforms in teaching methods over the last century; at each stage similar problems were also clearly demonstrated in the development of artistic concepts and creative techniques. Indeed, ever since Western art "came in" to China, it has had the effect of simultaneously and continuously inspiring, mingling, influencing and even replacing creative art and art education. When there is a certain type of artist, often there is a certain type of art education; if there is a certain type of art pedagogy, it inevitably gives rise to certain aesthetic values. The blame for whatever limitations there are in our aesthetic perceptions must lie alongside similar limitations in our art pedagogy; above all, this kind of situation in the teaching of art may arise from the fact that artists are creating works that are restricted by similar limitations. The development and achievements of our modern art can also be considered as the development and the achievements of our country's own art education. The presence of controversies surrounding Chinese modern art may be related to controversies in the art education system itself. They are so closely linked, so difficult to distinguish, that this situation may well be the source of malpractice in all our art education and artistic creation.

In China, artistic creation is often deemed to be the equivalent of art pedagogy; artists are expected to become pedagogues or take up teaching posts. Their double mission is to create art and teach art—a big responsibility. However, few of them realize that they will be taking on two types of duty; very few people are able to clearly differentiate between the dissimilar natures of these two issues even if they wanted to. In too many situations, this is treated as one and the same problem. At the moment, this is the biggest difference between our art education and that in other countries. So, in the history of modern art in China, as one of those rare individuals who have both shouldered responsibilities and carried out duties, Wu Guanzhong is recognized as being at once resilient, remarkable and outstanding.

In the world of art pedagogy, Wu Guanzhong worked tirelessly, assiduously and conscientiously as a teacher to the benefit of a whole generation of students, giving back to the education system far more than he had ever deserved to receive. As a young man, the excellent grounding he received in quality art education initially introduced him through his own experience to the irresistible attractions of creative art and how it can transform people's lives. Later on, his studies in the West gave him an early opportunity to realize how the concepts of contemporary art influenced pedagogy, with the enormous effect of harmony and wellbeing it exercises on human nature; once he became a teacher, he was then rapidly able to put into practice his progressively mature principles of art pedagogy and continue to encourage the spread of his teaching methods more widely. His principle was: art is an enterprise using the sense of sight to transform and establish an appreciation of beauty in the human mind; it is not just a job that relies on technique, training regulations or instruction methods.

Being an artist himself, Wu Guanzhong was clearly aware of the arduous and difficult process of creating an art work, knowing that these challenges arise not only in the search for and the use of the relevant method of artistic expression, but even more so from the hardship and perplexity a young person experiences during his attempts to achieve his own strongly individual aesthetic judgement and critical faculty. He never suggested that students should try to perfect their talents by referring to the great works bequeathed to us by our predecessors, neither did he encourage students to seek shortcuts by relying on the flotsam and jetsam of other people's success. What he proposed was always the students' own ingenuous imagination, the simple colours and forms of the students' perception, the awkward figures and shapes from the students' own hands. What he encouraged was that, never trying to reproduce nature; bravely creating from personal inspiration; promoting a personal sense harmony; always avoiding imitation of the past; rejecting suspicion of the West; developing motifs from ancient times and from abroad; being those who weave together the rich threads of the modern and the ethnic primitive.

In the position of being both an artist and a teacher, Wu Guanzhong was very clear about the similarities and differences in thought and method regarding creative painting and art education; and he was very clear about how a teacher should lead students to manage similarities and treat differences. He never arbitrarily used the style of an individual artwork in place of an art teaching method, nor did he ever put rigid rules of art pedagogy in the way of students' creative process. He was always aware that although art teaching is about the teacher and student undertaking an art work, it cannot be undertaken via the methods entailed in such an art work, and particularly not via the method used by a particular artist. He asked for recognition of the practical general aspects of art teaching and also promoted the individual nature of creative art. He always upheld the necessity for tolerance in the teaching process, and supported the pursuit of the creative process to its furthest limits. In the practice of art, he led the way into the fray, preaching by examples and helping the student to avoid the danger of losing his or her way in a thicket of constant repetition. Over more than half a century of the history of art pedagogy in China, innumerable students and artists benefitted from Wu Guanzhong's wise teaching; those who listened respectfully to his advice would all, to differing degrees, have become aware of his originality and how he stood out from the crowd.

Because Wu Guanzhong became our teacher, we became conscious of the existence of the close but unclear boundaries between form and content in painting, and in consequence this encouraged us to think. Because Wu Guanzhong took up pedagogy, we learned about modernism in painting and its enormous significance in each of our lives as artists, even rediscovering Cezanne and acquiring a fresh understanding of Van Gogh, even to the extent of enriching our understanding of others and ourselves. Because Wu Guanzhong took up pedagogy, we were part of a group who established their own aesthetic values, so that classes in aesthetics could be the key link in the art pedagogy that is still included in the art school syllabus. Because Wu Guanzhong took up pedagogy, art teaching is now no longer seen as a Subordinate of creative art and is now always considered as one of the tools to help artists learn their craft. It is becoming an increasingly independent discipline in accordance with the scientific standards in the domain. It is also because Wu Guanzhong took up pedagogy, that many teachers who have been enlightened by his wisdom are currently engaged in dedicated thinking on the subject, thus passing on art skills and art pedagogy by enabling students to develop into strong and well-balanced people rather than qualified standard instruments. Many of his open-minded students benefitted from the illumination of his teaching and came to think in a serious and conscientious way, their study of art thus developing a new awareness of the possibilities of thought, encouraging them to make independent choices. In the world of art everyone knows about the accomplishments of Wu Guanzhong as an artist. In the same way, as a pedagogue and teacher of art, through his energy and determination he had great success at a national level in the field of art education. In the history of art education in our country, Wu Guanzhong was a treasure for pedagogues, a treasure for art teaching, a treasure for our country.

重要的观看

我们能够看到的只是与事物相关的"物体",而不是事物本身。观看就是去看到那些存在于物体之间的我们看不见的事物,这个事物就是物质与物质间的关联。艺术是以呈现不可见的事物为特长的。我们能够看到的仅仅是事物的表象,但是看不到在表象之间存在的各种丰富的、多样的、有趣的、无穷无尽的相互关联。任何事物之间都存在着比较:形状的比较、色彩的比较、方向的比较、强弱的比较,等等。因为彼此不同,所以形成了差异;因为有所差异;才会产生必要的依赖和联系,才会形成描绘这种联系的方式和载体,形成运用这种方式和载体去传达思想和感情的行为,这个行为我们把它称作关于艺术的活动。

有些事物我们能够看到,有些事物我们不能够看到却能够感受到,有些事物我们既不能看到也不能感受到,但我们可以领悟到,因为我们还有比感觉能力更加敏锐的另一种能力,那就是灵性。依靠"灵性之智"我们能看到的更多,能感受到的更多,同时也能理解和辨别到更多。观看的意义在于"观"而不在于"看",绝对的"看"或者"不看"都是盲目的、被动的、狭隘的,是对存在于我们视觉范围之外的、包括我们自身价值在内的"主观事物"的否定和遗忘。在失去"主观价值"后,对于"客观事物"进行描绘、拍摄、选取的价值和意义也将不复存在。

　　艺术中的"观看"更多是指"领悟"，是所见、所听、所触、所思、所感、所觉的天然集成。在"观看"中呈现的事物，应该是相对的而不是绝对的。一双"相对观看"的眼睛，要比另一双"绝对观看"的眼睛更敏锐；一个相对意义上的蓝天，远比一个绝对意义上的蓝天更加灿烂。

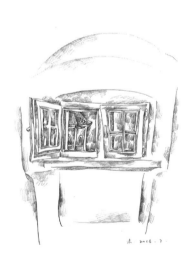

Perception of What Is Important

What we are able to see is merely the "concrete" part of things, but not their intrinsic substance. So perception is being able to see what exists in the embodiment of what we can't see: this thing is the substance and the links within that substance. The specificity of art is its ability to display the unseen. What we do see is only representation of things, but what we can't see are all the different sorts of rich, varied, fascinating and limitless reciprocal links that exist between these representations. Comparisons can always be formulated between things: comparisons of form, color, direction, strength, etc.; but because they do not mirror each other exactly, they begin to diverge. From this divergence, inevitable interdependence and connections arise; only then is it possible to use paint to give shape and weight to these relationships, for the implementation of this form and weight to transmit ideas and emotions and for us to use this in our creative work.

There are some things that we can see and there are some things that although we cannot see them, we can experience and sense them; there are some things we can neither see nor feel but that we can comprehend because we have another ability for emotion embedded in a different perceptive ability and that is sensitivity. On the basis of "sensitivity wisdom" we can perceive more, experience more, at the same time we can understand, discuss and compare more. The significance of perception is in the "observing" rather than the "seeing". Absolute "seeing" or "not seeing" are equally blind, passive and narrow; they exist beyond the scope of our vision, including the denial and loss of our own personal values towards "subjective things". When we lose "subjective values" where "objective things" are concerned, the values and significance of painting, photography or choice, cease to exist.

The "perceiving" in art is mostly "taking it in", it is the natural assimilation of what we see, hear, touch, think, feel and perceive. The things that are manifested during "perceiving" are necessarily relative and are not absolute. One pair of "relatively perceiving" eyes must be more perspicacious than another pair of "absolutely perceiving" eyes; a blue sky in a relative sense is far more brilliant than a blue sky in an absolute sense.

木. 2016. 7

判断的困难

判断是一种烦恼，因为没有唯一的标准，所以它让人很犹豫。判断是一种纠结，因为没有绝对的是非，所以它让人很困惑。判断是一种计较，因为没有永远的得失，所以它让人很无奈。放弃判断我们会远离这一切，放弃判断我们会感到麻木般的放纵！判断是一种愉悦，因为没有唯一的标准，所以才需要寻找自己的标准。判断是一种拓展，因为没有绝对的是非，所以才有可能让我们独立地面对是非。判断是一种责任，因为没有永远的得失，所以才会让我们忘却利益而追求意义。学会判断我们会拥有这一切，开始判断我们会感到未曾有过的振奋般的轻松。

判断是一种思考、一种由思考所引发的自主思维的习惯，并最终演变成独立的思考。没有思考的习惯，独立思考也就没有了可能。思考得越多，我们的独立性就越强；独立性越强，独特的、自我的、不同的判断结果才会产生，这样的判断结果，我们才可以称之为思想。

判断也是一种文化，一种个人、社会都无法回避的文化。判断得越多，文化也就越强大，反之则越弱小。个人的虚弱来自对判断的放弃，社会的虚弱则导致对文化的放弃。没有判断能力的个人是可怜的，没有判断能力的社会不仅是可怜的，而且是可悲的和可鄙的。

判断是一种义务和使命，一种对生命的繁衍的义务，一种对命运抗争的使命。在生命面前我们履行自己的义务，在命运面前我们承担自己的使命。丧失义务的生命没有任何价值，丧失使命的命运没有丝毫的意义，而所有这一切都是从丧失判断开始的。

The Difficulty of Judgement

Making an aesthetic judgement is a bit of a bother, because there is no single standard, it makes people very hesitant. Making a judgement is a bit of a muddle, as there is no absolute right or wrong, people get very confused. Making a judgement provokes argument: it brings no absolute profit or loss, so it makes people feel helpless. Giving up on judgement means distancing oneself from all such disturbance, which means becoming comfortably insensitive! Somehow though, formulating a judgement is really satisfying: there is no single standard, so one has to seek one's own standard. Judgement leaves room for scope, as there is no absolute gain or loss, it means facing up to ones own rights or wrongs. Making a judgement also implies responsibility, as there is no permanent gain or loss, we tend to forget about self-interest in order to find meaning. Raising our own awareness of judgement means that we can do all these things and then we realise that we have never felt so relaxed and positive.

Forming a judgement is a thinking process, a sort of habit arising from self-possessed reflection, eventually evolving to become personal awareness. If one is not used to thinking, then there is no possibility of personal awareness. It is only through deep reflection that one's individuality becomes stronger, more pronounced, and then individual, personal, differing judgements can effectively take shape. It is only this effective judgement that can be qualified as thought.

Judgement is a sort of culture; the sort of culture that no person or society can possibly avoid. The more people are conscious of aesthetic judgement, the stronger their culture, otherwise culture becomes shaky. Individual weakness comes from abandoning a sense of judgement, and societal weakness stems from abandoning culture. It's a pity when individuals lack the ability to judge; it's not only a pity when society lacks judgement, it's a tragedy.

In a way, judgement is a sort of task and mission, a set of multiple duties towards life, and a way to resist the progress of fate. In life we can carry out our duties, in the meantime, shoulde take up the mission that fate lays in our way. A life that loses its obligations has no value; a fate that loses its mission has little significance; and when that happens we begin to lose awareness of the value of judgement.

朩、2016.7.

可贵的参与

艺术从参与开始，并且以不再参与而告终。当我们更多、更深、更广泛地参与到事物的相互关联当中时，与此相关的规则、规律、状态、意义、性质以及所形成的各种问题就会不断地被连带和显现出来；而对于这些问题的思考、探究、试验则是艺术最应该做的事情。

作为一种过程，一种不计较功能、不计较利益、不计较得失和结果的过程，参与是崇高的。作为一种结果，当"所有的结果都变为过程"成为结果的时候，参与是实在的。作为一种浪漫，一种能随时随地获得的惊喜和沮丧，一种并不随心所欲的允许融入和游离，参与是理想的，而理想对任何社会的人们都是最最重要的。

思维的参与和行为的参与构成了参与的整体，思维与行为状态界定的不确定性，使得参与活动本身具有了天然的"非秩序性"和"非规律性"。无论参与本身的方式是怎样的不同，我们都能够从中获得无尽的精神充实与无尽的快乐体验，而无须以能力、身份、职业、资历作为依据，也无须以时间、空间、价值取向作为前提。

参与作为一种事实上的审美活动体验，是所有人天经地义的和不可取代的生活权利和社会义务。放弃参与等同于放弃社会生活以及放弃自我，我们不可以承受这种放弃的代价。

参与还意味着对开明的认同、对多元的认同、对宽容的认同，而所有这些认同恰恰也是对艺术的认同，因为对艺术的参与过程也就是对艺术的认同过程。

Worthwhile Participation

Art began with people taking part, and if participation is not continually renewed then that's the end of it. At the very time when we are taking part more frequently, intensely and extensively in the interconnections at the heart of things, all the various questions relating directly to regulations, rules, attitudes, significance continue to become apparent; then the study, research and experiment in these areas are all urgent and essential activities of art.

As a process, a sort of informal, disinterested, discalculated process, taking part is an honourable and creditable commitment. As an outcome, when "all results transform into process" becomes the result, participation becomes a reality. As a sort of Romanesque ideal, a sort of unexpected approbation or discouragement constantly received from all quarters, and a sort of equivocal permissible harmony and isolation, participation is akin to an ideal and for people, whatever their social context, the ideal is really, really important.

Participation in thought and participation in action together form; the scope of these thoughts and actions has no clearly defined limits thus, the appropriate participative action itself is naturally "without command structure" and "without rulebooks". The mode of participation itself is bound to be diverse, but we can all achieve both endless enrichment of spirit and endless experience of happiness from it. It is not necessary to use ability, status or competence as a basis, nor is it necessary to use time, space or value as a premise.

As an aspect of making aesthetic judgement, by the fact of being alive, taking part is everyone's basic and irreplaceable right and their social obligation. Abandoning things like participation is like abandoning one's existence in society and giving up on oneself, which comes at too high a cost.

Taking part already implies the endorsement of enlightenment, differentiation and tolerance, all corresponding to an endorsement of art, because by endorsing participation in making art works, one endorses the artistic process itself.

最终的选择

艺术说到底就是选择：不是选择物质，因为在物质与物质之间我们无从选择；不是选择精神，因为我们从来都是被精神选择而不是选择精神；不是选择内容，因为对于内容的选择往往形同于没有选择；不是选择形式，因为形式的确立并不是来源于选择，而是来源于实践和创造。选择的对象只有一个，就是自我。选择说到底就是艺术，无论是绘画的艺术、音乐的艺术、建筑的艺术、设计的艺术，还是领导的艺术、战争的艺术、烹饪的艺术，都是在选择中确立与存在的。

有选择才有所放弃，才有所保留；有选择才有果断，才有优柔；有选择才有成功，才有失败；有选择才有挑战，才有超越；有选择才有创造，才有自信，才有对于艺术最最重要的刺激和好奇。

选择不是赌博，而是对未曾发生的事情所做的决定，是对随后发生的事情所要做的承诺。

选择不是冒险，尽管选择本身具有风险，但对于风险的承担正是选择的价值所在。选择不完全是理性的抉择，绝对的理性分析在复杂化、多样化、个性化的面前缺乏说服力。选择也不完全是感性的寄托，绝对的感性主导会使本已不确定的因素更加不确定。

选择是一种理想，能够按照自己的愿望和意志做出选择的人毫无疑问是幸运的，哪怕这种选择只有一次。

选择是一种自我超越，一种跨过已有的束缚并向着未知的吸引前进的超越。选择是一种救赎，一种用"沉浸在既有的习惯中享乐的堕落"去换取"不顾代价地奔向崭新归宿"的救赎。

选择之所以痛苦，在于被选择的事物的不可知，以及潜在的失败。选择之所以艰难，在于它永远没有前车之鉴，需要学会将一切重头做起。选择之所以快乐，在于它赋予你做出决定的机遇，以及所带来的决定后的期待。选择之所以荣耀，在于它敦促我们通过每一次的选择而变得自信、自立和自强。

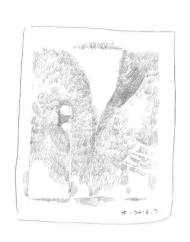

Finalizing Choices

Art is really about choices. It's not about choosing substance, because we cannot make a choice between one substance and another. It's not about making a spiritual choice, because it's the spirit that chooses us and not the other way around. It's not a question of choosing content, because as far as content goes, choosing it or not choosing it tends to be the same thing. It's not about establishing shape, because it does not come from choosing but from implementation and creativity. There is only one possible partner for choice and that is the self. So making choices is the basis of art; it doesn't matter whether it's the art of painting, or music, or architecture, or decoration, or whether it's the art of leadership, battle or cuisine: these things occur and come about due to choices.

Only once there has been a choice can there be interruption or perseverance; with choice there can then be determination or indecision; when choice is available only then can one opt for success or failure, only then can one opt to contest or to overcome; it is only when there is choice that there can be creativity, confidence, and those most vitally important elements towards the arts: enthusiasm and curiosity.

Choosing is not a game of chance. It is a decision concerning something that hasn't happened yet; it is a commitment to something that will come about later on.

Choice doesn't imply exposing oneself to danger, although in itself choice implies exposure to risk. However, the presence of risk is really where the value of choice lies. Choosing is never a completely rational decision; entirely rational analysis can be unconvincing when complications, diversification and individualization need to be taken into account. Neither is choice really the place for sentiment, but absolute control over the emotions may have the effect of reinforcing a tendency to indecision.

Choice is a sort of ideal and those who can make a choice according to their own desires and determination are certainly very lucky, even if it only occurs once in a lifetime. Making choices is a way of excelling oneself, developing to face the unknown and captivating future. Choice is a sort of redemption: a way to exchange the "succumbing to sybaritic degeneration through habit" token for the "moving towards a bright new destination whatever the cost" card.

The source of the pain that may be involved in choosing lies in the unknowable outcome, in the potential for failure. The reason for the difficulty involved in choosing is that no one ever learns from the failures of others, and everyone has to learn everything from scratch. The reason for the joy involved in choice resides in the fact that it provides the pleasure the decision may bring and the enjoyable expectancy of the outcome. The wonderful thing about choosing is that it encourages us to become more confident, independent and accomplished every time we make a choice.

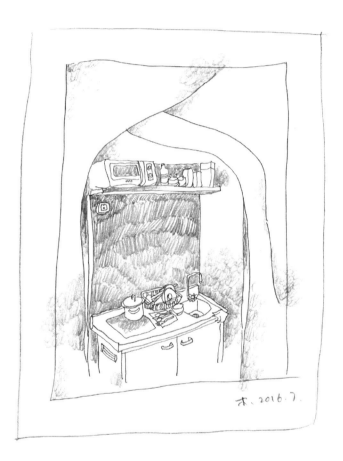

木、2016.7.

获得与失去同样值得尊敬

"获得"还是"失去",虽不像"生存还是毁灭"那般绝对,但也还是界定出在艺术选择状态中取舍观念的差异与极端。极端是肯定的,要么得到,要么失去,二者必居其一。谁会拒绝更多的在艺术的过程中具体的"获得"呢——创作的快乐、成功的喜悦、物质的回报,等等?而二者的差异则未必:在我们得到的同时是否又失去了很多呢?

永远快乐的快乐是否可以称其为快乐?创作的持续成功何以称其为成功?至于所有性质的回报又有哪一项无须付出和没有代价?相反地,"失去"又何尝不是一种"获得"?创作上的困扰仍不失为一种愉悦;成就的本身就意味着事物的终结;物质的增加必然导致精神的减少。因此,"获得"与"失去"在本质上并没有什么不同。在艺术创作的过程中我们应该对它们报以同样的真诚,因为"获得"与"失去"这两个概念本身都值得尊敬。

我们"获得"的喜悦应是劳作之后的思量,我们"失去"的困惑应作为下一次"失去"之前的"获得"。创作的方式与方法没有积极或消极的区别,画面的好坏也不是判断我们得失的准则。我们希望顺利,也同样希望艰辛能带来努力。局部与整体的"把握"不是艺术基础能力必须要有的:我们关注整体的效果,也考虑局部的利益,但归根结底是创作者自己的局部和整体，真正的"把握"是因人而异的。

绘画的目的在于判断，得与失的判断是重要的判断，"获得"也可能是一种"失去"。艺术的意义在于思考，取与舍的思考是主要的思考，"失去"也能够是一种"获得"。

Balancing Respect for Achievement and Failure

The difference between "achievement" and "failure" in painting is not like the stark opposition of "to be or not to be", but it still indicates the wide range of attitudes that are involved in making judgements about art. Extremes stand out clearly, but irrespective of whether success or rejection is at stake, a choice has to be made. During the artistic process, who can possibly deny the existence of real "achievement" in concrete terms when painting involves the joy of creativity, the pleasure of success, material reward, etc.? But is such a clear divide between achievement and failure really necessary? As one reaps reward, doesn't he or she also lose a certain concomitant something?

Can a permanent state of happiness really be called happiness? How can succeeding in being continuously productive be called success? As to the rewards of quality, can there possibly be intangible returns with no price to pay? And can the flipside of "messing up" not be considered to be some sort of "making good"? The challenges and difficulties involved in creating can still be a source of satisfaction. Achievement really means completing a work, while greater preoccupation with material things entails an evident decline in the spiritual aspect. So it follows that in essence "making good" and "losing out" have something in common. During the artistic process our attitudes in responding to both have to be balanced, because the concepts of "making good" and "losing out" find their own equilibrium.

The satisfaction that artists "reap" is experienced in the

post-completion pondering on the work; this is when "foregoing" or eliminating any doubts becomes the "gain" before the next "loss". Manners and methods for being creative cannot be differentiated as either positive or negative; furthermore, the good or bad in painting are not what establish the criteria for achievement or failure. We would like our work to go well, and similarly we also look forward to testing our capacity for effort. Partial or total "grasp" is not what is needed for the basic task of art: we need to pay attention to the entire effect and at the same time study the relative weight of the parts. But in the end, it is only by taking into account both the separate elements and the whole character of the creative artists themselves while respecting people's differences that we can have a true "grasp".

The purport of painting lies in the forming of an opinion. Judging the importance of what to reap and what to forego becomes essential when "gain" can also be a form of "loss". The significance of art lies in thought; concentrating on what to obtain and what to leave aside becomes a meditative exercise, and "foregoing" may well be seen as a sort of "harvest".

本. 2016.7.

控制与失控同样珍贵

绘画的本质就是"控制"与"反控制"、"放任"与"坚持"间的博弈：表面上看，是人与艺术作品间的抗衡。要么你"控制"它，要么你被它所"控制"。要么你希望"失控"，要么你放弃"失控"，不是成功便是失败。

而在思想层面上看，控制与放手是人类精神境界中不同意识间的抗衡，是人类本性之中感性与理性间的冲突，说到底是放任与束缚之间的斗争。我们的本意是放任，而我们的理智却要制约我们的放任，因为前者属于自我因素，后者则属于社会因素。我们需要在其中选择，既需要顾此，又不要失彼。

这不仅是艺术，同时也是生活，这也是艺术本质上所具有的乐趣和挑战所在。"失去控制"作为美学意义中的一种观点，提示人们在"实施控制"的同时，反思相反意义的价值所在，因为控制不能是永无休止的和永无节制的。"放弃控制"与"反对控制"截然不同，前者是有所自觉的境界，后者是有所被迫的无奈。作为艺术创作过程中的积极手段，"放手"同样占有时间上和空间上的优势，它占尽了显性和隐性的双重资源，进可以攻，退可以守，大有以逸待劳、四两拨千斤之功效，只不过多数人并没有意识到它的价值所在罢了。

Control and Letting Go

The nature of painting is "control" and "opposing control", or a match between "letting go" and "hanging on" : on the surface it seems like a contest between people and their artwork. Either you are in "control" of it, or it is in "control" of you. Whether you're hoping to "lose control" or whether you give up on "losing control", not succeeding either way underlines the loss.

In the mind, being in control and letting go represent the dichotomy between two states of consciousness battling over the territories of emotion and reason in the human psyche, ultimately creating a tension between being indulgent and exercising restraint. Our primary intention is towards indulgence, but reasoning tends to restrict indulgence. Being indulgent is a personal factor and the restraint is a social matter. We are obliged to make a choice, and although we opt to strike a deal with one, we don't want to lose out on the other.

It's not just about art, at the same time it's about life; it's about the place at the very core of the nature of art where both pleasures and challenges lie. "Letting go" as a concept with aesthetic significance means that while people are "applying control", they are also considering the value of rejecting it, because control cannot be endless and excessive. The notions of "foregoing control" and "opposing control" are not the same thing; the former involves self-imposed limits; the latter concerns an external restraint. As a positive means of the creative artistic process, "letting go" is also much better as far as both time and space are concerned; it uses both evident and subjacent resources, progressing or retreating, often standing at ease, and with the effect of a substantial payoff from a small investment. But many people are unaware of its benefits...

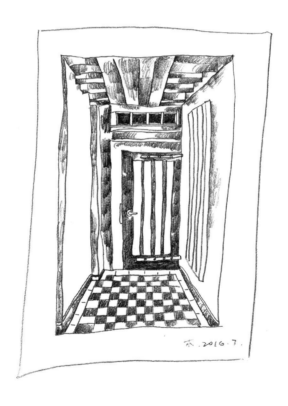

完善与不完善同样有价值

一幅完善的画并不意味着应该被全部画满，或者说画到没得可画的东西为止。完善与否的概念不能等同于构图的均衡，也不能等同于画面深入程度的多少。完善不是一个僵化的概念或标准，它是我们判断造型规律的方法和手段。初学者的造型不能完善，因为他们将完善理解得过于具体，以至于用完善强行掩盖了他们的不完善。

熟练者的造型很完善，因为他们为了完善而完善，以至于他们忘记了不完善的珍贵与创作上的可能性。其实完善与不完善同样是一对矛盾的综合体，天底下任何一件艺术作品如果无懈可击、十全十美，那它本身就是不完善的。完善的事物从理论上讲，一般都是精心谋划、千锤百炼的产物，它的核心价值就在于"运筹与熟练"。

然而这一点也是造型艺术的大忌，因为它扼杀了艺术相对性中不可知和偶然性的一面，而片面地强调它的必然性与可控性的另一面，让造型艺术堕入僵化、规范、概念的深渊。不完善的事物虽然有着许多先天的不足和后天的遗憾，但它留给创作者的余地却是无限的，它使得造型的过程从开始到结束充满了猜想和挑战。完善与不完善之间既不是冤家对头，也不可以是亲朋好友，它们是相互转变的、不同效果的、不可分离的事物的两个方面。有许多的艺术作品以不完善开始，以完善告终，也有许多的艺术作品是以完善起始，却以不完善终结。

还有更多的艺术作品从始至终都是不完善的，但是它们的艺术魅力并没有因此而受到丝毫的影响。也许我们不应忽视不完善的作用，至少应该一视同仁才对。

Making It Perfect Isn't the Point

A perfectly complete painting doesn't mean filling in all the space and painting right up to the edges, or that you didn't stop until all the things that could be included are actually there on the canvas. The notion of whether a work is really finished cannot be considered in the same way as balance in composition, or be on the same footing as depth of scope. Perfection is not a rigid concept or standard but one of the ways to judge the creative arts. The stuff produced by novice students can't be perfectly complete because they comprehend perfection in terms of their materials, just concentrating on "finish" to disguise their lack of completion.

The work of experienced artists is perfect, because their target is to be perfect. So the importance of the incompletement and its potential of the creative process are ignored. In fact completion and incompleteness are the twin elements of a paradox: wherever it is on this Earth, if an artwork cannot be criticised and is considered perfect, then something of its substance is incomplete. In theory, things that are perfect are generally the product of meticulous design and hard grind, with their core value resting in careful preparation and constant exercise of technique.

However, seeking perfection is the great pitfall of creative art, because it stifles awareness of potential and of the unforeseen in artistic relativism. On the other hand the quest for "perfect" also leads the way towards the attendant inevitable and controllable, allowing creative art to stumble into an abyss of rigidity and standardisation. Although the incomplete work may create an impression of yesterday's unfinished canvas and regret for the potential tomorrow, it provides the artist with endless space, with the possibilities and challenges following a putative creative process from start to finish. There isn't a love-hate relationship between the finished painting and the unfinished work, nor are they really close friends; the pair are mutually transformative but they do not produce the same effect nor can they be isolated as separate phenomena. There are many artistic works that have an incomplete beginning and a complete conclusion, and there are many works of art that have a complete beginning and an incomplete end.

There are still even more art works that are imperfect from start to finish, but this in no way affects their artistic charm. Perhaps we should not neglect the role of imperfection; at the very least it is only fair that we regard it with respect.

构建与破坏同样重要

构建的同时也要考虑破坏，这听上去似乎不可思议，但构建始于破坏是毋庸置疑的逻辑。往往我们在开始构筑的同时，破坏也就开始了。也许我们只考虑了从无到有的结果，而未曾考虑从无到有的过程。结果是收获，过程又何尝不是收获？

结果让我们看到了建构；过程让我们体会了破坏与构建的相互依存。空间的塑造或非塑造，色彩的描绘或非描绘，每一笔、每一画的过程都包含了构建与破坏的双重意义与关联，一个因素刚刚确立，随即被另一个因素替代；一个形象刚刚完成，随即被另一个形象所取代。我们很难界定出哪一个因素和形象是构建，哪一个因素或形象是破坏。建构与破坏的高度统一才是艺术创作的永恒真谛。我们都知道"不破不立"的道理：破字当头，立也就在其中。

相反亦然："不立不破"，立字当头，破也就在其中。只一味地做叠加而不做相应的舍弃，只知道数量的增加带来的乐趣、而不知本质的提升不以数量的增减为前提的人和机构，是不可能在创作上有所造诣的。

在造型艺术领域，我们需要构建，且将构建作为艺术的终极目标并为之努力；但我们不要忘记，伴随着建构的还有破坏以及由破坏所引发的对于建构的理性思考。从此意义上讲，破坏要比汇总重要得多，也比汇总的意义积极得多。建构与破坏可以同时是因，也可以同时是果。

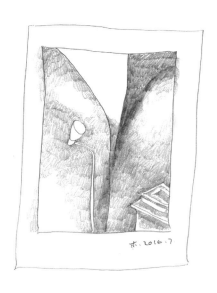

Putting Together and Dismantling

It appears to be nonsensical to say that you should think about how things come apart while you are putting them up, but in fact it is perfectly logical to start building on a demolition site. Often while we are starting to put something together, we have also embarked on the process of taking apart. Maybe at the outset we just aimed at achieving results without considering the process of how we actually get there. If the result is positive, doesn't the process also return some kind of gain?

The result allows us to perceive the construction; the process allows us to learn by experience about the interdependence of taking apart and putting together. Shaping a space or not shaping it, painting with colours or not using them; the process of every effective brushstroke contains the paired significance and connection between putting together and taking apart. As soon as one element has been clearly established, it is replaced by another component. As soon as an image is created, another takes its place. It is very difficult to determine the extent to which each element or shape is built up and which is deleted. The true meaning of creative art lies in the integration of construction and deconstruction. We all know the popular saying "no breaking, no making" — the taking apart comes first with the potential for putting together already presents.

And vice versa, when we say "no making, no breaking", construction comes first and when it begins, the seeds of destruction are held within it. When paint is continually piled on but nothing is appropriately eliminated; when success is measured simply in rising numbers, but where there is no awareness of the fact that true aesthetic development does not depend on set production rates, neither the academic institutional bodies concerned nor the people within them are capable of achieving artistic accomplishment.

In the field of the creative arts, we must build, making putting together the ultimate aim of our art and our creative effort; but we must not forget that along with the construction there is dismantling and its attendant reasoning and reflection on the construction. In this sense, taking apart is more important than putting together, and has much more positive significance. At the same time, as both the constructive and the destructive can be cause, they can also both be effect.

村上 2016.7.

想好了再画还是画好了再想

这个对大多数人来说似乎不是问题的问题，现在却成了最大的问题。绘画正在变得越来越像某种设计，人人都要"想好了再画"，生怕画得不好。

没人愿意"画好了再想"，因为那已没有意义。"想好了再画"，可以借助人们的经验，可以把握绘画的方式、方向和进程，最重要的是可以不再付出思考的努力，不再承受失败的压力，一切都是现成的，只是结果的程度不同罢了。但"成竹在胸"的最好结果也只能是"竹子"，没有其他。而"画好了再想"就不同了，它需要面对每一次不尽相同的挑衅：画到什么程度才结束，要根据每一次的具体情况来确定；以往的经验和技巧也许不再有效，至少不完全有效。每张作品的结果都是未知的，创作者为此要承受失败的痛苦，要感受到自信心所受到的伤害，也许还会因此而放弃创作。但是他们终究还是自由的、自在的，他们可以无拘无束地去画，并且无拘无束地去想。他们可以感受到绘画过程所带来的快乐，他们还可以在自己有限的绘画中体验到艺术创作的无限。

这类人是艺术活动中的少数，同时也是艺术发展的潜力和希望。说到底能够称为艺术的东西，从本质上说都应该是这个世界上没有出现过的新东西，无论它们是色彩还是形状；至于是不是"好的色彩"或"好的形状"，那是下一步的事。

Think It Out and then Paint?

For many people, this question is not considered to be a problem, but it has become the greatest issue of our time. The current trend is that painting is in the process of becoming more like designing in that people want to "think it out and then paint", because they are worried about making a bad painting.

Nobody wants to "complete a painting and then think it out", because that would be meaningless. "Think it out and then paint" can help people to gain experience; it can help them to manage style, direction and process in painting. The most important thing is that it saves reinvesting in the effort of reflection and avoids the pressure of failure, because the result is ready-made, but the quality of that result is not the same. Even the best work built on "an intimate knowledge of bamboo" can only be "bamboo", and not anything else. Whereas "painting and then thinking it out" is quite different, it has to face challenges repeatedly: what quality of painting must be achieved, according to what background is each painting evaluated; whether previous experience and skills are still effective, or at least whether they still have full effect. The result of every painting is unknown, thus artists have to endure the pain of failure, suffer damage to their self-confidence, and it may even lead to abandoning a painting. But eventually they can become free and at ease, painting without hindrance and thinking without constraint. They can experience the pleasure that the process of painting brings and they can also, within the bounds of their own painting, become conscious of the limitless expanse of the arts.

There are not many people in the arts who achieve this, but at the same time they represent the potential and the aspirations for future development. Basically what can be called art in essense, should be those new things that have not appeared in the world, whether that be colour or shape. And as to whether they are "good colours" or "good shapes" is another story.